Mark Wheeller

Race To Be Seen

Graham – World's Fastest Blind Runner.

Developed to tell the story of Mark's original play written with Epping Youth Theatre 1983.

Original underscore soundtrack by Danny Sturrock remixing the original songs from *Race to Be Seen* by Graham Salmon, Mark Wheeller and Steve Wyatt.

Salamander Street

PLAYS

Developed from Mark Wheeller's original stage play *Race To Be Seen* written with the Epping Youth Theatre and originally published as *Race To Be Seen* by the Epping Forest District Council in 1984 and Longmans in 1986.
©1984 & 1986 Mark Wheeller

Graham – World's Fastest Blind Runner developed from *Race* and was premiered by the Eastleigh Borough Youth Theatre at the Edinburgh Festival Fringe 2001 and published by dbda. This led to a further edited version premiered by Oaklands Youth Theatre and subsequently published by dbda.

©2001 & 2008 Mark Wheeller.

Race To Be Seen 2021 definitive edition © 2021 Mark Wheeller

Published in 2021 by Salamander Street Ltd.
(info@salamanderstreet.com)

ISBN: 9781913630867

10 9 8 7 6 5 4 3 2 1

For Marie Salmon, in loving memory of Graham Salmon MBE (my Storybook Man) 1952–1999.

CONTENTS

Acknowledgements

The writing and researching team from Epping Youth Theatre 1983:

Matthew Allen; Lisa Beer; Zara Chapman; Frances Jackson; Barrie Sapsford.

Assisted by:

Dawn Baker; Bernadette Chapman; Laura Dove; Jan Farrindon; Nicki Harris; Jonathon Hicks; Rebecca Mallison; Paddy Mallison; Luke Nyman; Sara Record; Alis Stylianou; Tracy Tee & Steve Wyatt.

Sources:

Graham & Marie Salmon.

Maud and Harry, Graham's mum and dad.

June & Susan, Graham's sisters.

The following are in alphabetical order:

Bill Aitken; John Anderson; John Bailey; Christine Baker *(Christiev Services)*; Mike Brace; Claude Charman; *Daily Mail*; Sandy Gray. *Guardian and Gazzette (Walthamstow)*, *The Guinness Book Of Records*; Brigitte Hall; Frank Matthews; Moorfields Eye Hospital; Ron Murray; Kath and Lew Pegg; Robert Phillip; Susie Rothwell; *Wide Eyed and Legless* Graham Salmon; Joyce Streetin, Keith Wells, Mark Wheeller, Roger Wray & Pete Young.

Danny Sturrock for the Music and Media.

Barrie Sapsford for maintaining his interest *(from his EYT days)* and helping to keep it alive through work on the DVD and associated book *Verbatim – The Fun Of Making Theatre Seriously* by Mark Wheeller, also published by Salamander Street.

Thanks also to the following productions which also substantially assisted to this definitive script.

OYT *(1987/2008)*

Tim Ford's EBYT *(2000)*

Cathy Hudson's Therwood School *(2007)*

Introduction

Graham Salmon MBE was a hero of mine along with David Bowie and George Best. However, Graham was a hero that I was fortunate enough to become friends with and as a result I was in the perfect position to tell his remarkable story!

Graham was my hero and he lived beyond my expectations of him. He was such a special person. So if I'm allowed to have a favourite play of mine, I often say it's *Race To Be Seen*. All of my plays are important to me but this is different. I have often wondered why it is not my best-known play. I think people were scared to stage the final climatic race scene. Although car accidents didn't seem to get in the way of *Too Much Punch* and *Chicken!,* both of which have had around 6,000 licensed performances as opposed to the meagre fifty-six this play has achieved.

It had a wonderful start. When Epping Youth Theatre first performed *Race To Be Seen,* they won plaudits on tour and at the Edinburgh Fringe. Perhaps, without the model of a professional company touring it, teachers just aren't aware of it? Perhaps it was because the 2001 edition of the dbda book had a song on the opening page? Perhaps it was because I hadn't explained how to stage it well enough in the stage directions… yet in other plays this has been described as a benefit? Perhaps it was the cover design?

I felt I was too close to it to put (the re-branded and more direct title) *Graham – World's Fastest Blind Runner* on myself. I was delighted when Tim Ford, then of Eastleigh Borough Youth Theatre, suggested that he would do so. I knew in allowing Tim to do it that the premiere was in good hands. He has since gone on to be a director at the prestigious Birmingham Rep and Litchfield Garrick, supporting my view of him as a most innovative and imaginative director. *Graham – World's Fastest Blind Runner* was Tim's first Edinburgh Fringe production which achieved similar plaudits to our 1984 production of *Race To Be Seen.* It was Critics' Choice for the Scottish Evening News.

Mike Fleetwood, the Drama teacher from Parkside College, used the play for his A Level group in 2006 and was quick to contact me when the results came through with the following message:

Mark,

Thought that you'd like to know that the Yr12 students who performed Graham as part of their AS level did exceptionally well. Overall, they achieved 5 grade A's and 2 grade B's! Even better than that was the breakdown of the unit marks and for Unit 2 i.e. the performance of 'Graham', they all got grade A's! Topping that though was the fact that all seven of them not only got the top grade for the performance but they were all awarded 100% for it; 120/120 marks! It's worth noting that the external moderator was accompanied that evening by her senior examiner also.

I didn't ever need convincing 'Graham' was an ideal piece to challenge my group. It ticked all the boxes for A level work, but if I ever needed justification, the results have certainly given it. Thanks again for the material and thanks to Graham, such an inspirational person!

This was the first time in years that anyone who had come to the play cold had given themselves the chance to be complimentary about it.

The next year I had a message from Cathy Hudson, Head of Drama at the Therwood School in Surrey, letting me know she was entering an edited version of the play into a Drama Festival. During the week of the Festival, she invited me to see the production as it was to be re-presented on the Saturday because it had won the Festival. Michael Caine was in attendance to present the awards. I decided to attend at very short notice and was absolutely knocked out. It was a truly original production. It was very differently staged to the way I had conceived it and pushed my thinking about the play forward significantly.

By this time I had made a decision to stage the play with my Oaklands Youth Theatre. This was something I thought I would never have done as it seemed arrogant to present a play featuring me in it! However a group of students in one of my GCSE classes had presented a well performed extract for their GCSE and helped me to overcome my concern. This coincided with a very real threat to OYT by an Academy take-over. I wanted something special to put on as a swan-song. *Race To Be Seen* suited this perfectly as I was so fond of it and it had been my inaugural production.

During my visit to see the Therwood production, which went on to be performed in the final of the National Drama Festivals Association (NDFA), I was already thinking about editing the play so we could use it in a One Act Play Festival but I was having trouble. This version was cut down to 25 minutes! It certainly gave me ideas and also some certainty about sections that I decided MUST stay in!

Oaklands Youth Theatre had won many awards in my 20 years there including a couple on a national platform. However, one that had eluded us was to win our local Totton Drama Festival despite nearly 20 entries!

Imagine my joy when we won with *Race To Be Seen* and were awarded four other awards as well! We went on through the rounds to represent our area in the English Final (above all the adult groups) and won the adjudicator's special award for our ensemble work. No one from the Totton Drama Festival had ever done this before (or since to date 2021). It was amazing!

It was now a proven Festival success two years in a row and I hoped would be noticed by other groups. This was helped in no small part by the fact that former EYT *Race To Be Seen* cast member, Barrie Sapsford, filmed the OYT production to make it available on DVD. This has been used successfully by many as a springboard for ideas so that the play can go on being developed. The DVD continues to be available from Salamander Street.

As a result of a growing appreciation of the play, I was asked to include a scheme of work for Edexcel in their GCSE exam resource book. This did bring some attention to the play for a short while… until the GCSE's were superseded and the book became effectively redundant. The excellent scheme of work is now available with some additional work by Tracy Dorrington to make it accessible in a world where online learning and social distancing might apply. It was one of my favourite schemes while I was at school.

How did my relationship with Graham begin? I first met Graham and Marie in 1983 after my then Youth Theatre (Epping in Essex) had decided to make Graham the subject of my very first documentary play. The story of *Race To Be Seen* is told briefly in the script but it would be suffice to say the project was incredibly successful. It lead to my first publishing contract with Longmans. It is also described in detail in my 2021 book *Verbatim – The Fun Of Making Theatre Seriously,* also available from Salamander Street.

The original *Race To Be Seen* opened many doors for me. Although that publication was unsuccessful in terms of sales, I knew there was a play in there waiting to get out. Sadly, it took Graham's death to inspire the next successful stage of this project with the full blessing of Marie, Graham's wife. She remains a regular and very welcome visitor (and spoiler of our children/grandchild in the nicest possible way) to our house.

There may be tragic moments in Graham's story but equally important is the humour and optimism of Graham himself. The person who plays Graham must be able to smile! He should wear an almost constant grin and deliver a "cheeky" attitude wherever possible. Graham was an inspiration to all who met him, so charisma is a key element. This is a role in a million and anyone taking it on will not forget Graham Salmon MBE. I know it has made a deep impression on all who have played him thus far.

I still think of Graham most days. Whenever I visited Graham's house I would spend time with him listening to music on his amazingly expensive Hi-Fi system. Sound was very important to him. His system could find depths in music I didn't know existed. When I returned to my house I'd listen to the same music on my standard (not bad) Hi-Fi system to cross reference. I never found these depths in my system.

Some years ago I took the first stages in upgrading my Hi-Fi. Now, whenever I put a CD (or record) on I think about Graham and I know he'd approve of my system. My wife always reminds me that by now Graham would have something even more amazing. I like to feel that I've nearly caught up with him on this score even though on a running track he left me for dead when I once agreed to do a warm up with him! It's strange how people remain in your life. To most who know of Graham he was an inspirational athlete. I quote from Robert Philip, the *Daily Telegraph* Sports Columnist:

Graham Salmon is the most inspiring athlete I have met; I say this without a moment's hesitation even though I have enjoyed the rare privilege of sharing the company of Muhammad Ali, Stanley Matthews, Gary Sobers, Martina Navratilova, Nadia Comaneci, Arnold Palmer and countless others in the course of my job.

There was so much more to him. More than even my play can communicate but in a nutshell; Graham was all you could want from a friend/hero with a wonderful sense of humour. He had an amazing Hi-Fi, oh yes, and a few world records oh, and he was totally blind too!

I had initially written *Graham – World's Fastest Blind Runner* for Marie, in the period after Graham passed away in 1999, not knowing if it would ever be produced on stage. It was something I felt I could do to mark his greatness. It became a turning point in my Youth Theatre career starting off an unbelievable run of successes in the All England Theatre Festival where OYT reached the final in three successive entries *(Graham, STOP THE TRAFFIK* and *Jack)*. When I retired from Youth Theatre work in 2018 I had not imagined making further alterations to the play then 2020 arrived with its unique qualities!

At the start of COVID-19 pandemic, my publisher (Dbda/Zinc) suddenly announced they were closing without any advance notice. Within a couple of days George Spender brought forward the date of opening his new independent theatre publishing company. He suggested he was willing to take on pretty much my complete back catalogue. This led to me having the opportunity to update all of my plays which I am now part way through achieving.

I was particularly pleased to be able to do this with *Graham*. One of the first decisions was to revert to the original title *Race To Be Seen*. In the original 1983 production, I felt we had focused on Graham the athlete. In the 2000 & 2008 productions, the focus shifted to Graham the man. In this, I have tried to make it more balanced and show Graham as a man in the context of what his legacy was for the Paralympics.

Central to this were the words of John Anderson, coach and host of TV show *Gladiators:*

The era of Britain winning gold medals in these games began with Graham Salmon in Bulgaria. He's an inspiration to everyone. Britain should be proud of him.

I was already writing my book about verbatim theatre with a particular focus on *Race To Be Seen* and *Graham – World's Fastest Blind Runner.* As part of my research, I watched all the productions on video/DVD. As I was watching, I made copious notes about sections that had gone missing from the later version and needed to be reinstated.

The 2021 *Race To Be Seen* is the definitive version. I cannot wait to see it in performance. Good luck to those who work on this play. Please get it performed and make people aware of Graham. I will be genuinely pleased to hear of your experiences when producing it and please, please, please send me any reviews or news of awards you get.

In loving memory of Graham, my "Storybook Man".

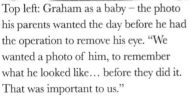

Top left: Graham as a baby – the photo his parents wanted the day before he had the operation to remove his eye. "We wanted a photo of him, to remember what he looked like… before they did it. That was important to us."

Bottom left: Graham set a new British high jump record for the totally blind at 1 metre 38… about neck height to an average adult.

Top right: Graham on his tricycle proudly posing for the local newspaper.

Bottom right: Graham training for the 1983 European Championships with his guide, Roger Wray

aham with a young Ben Shephard, who played the young Graham in the original
ping Youth Theatre production.

The amazing opportunities offered to a young performer who gets to play Graham Salmon

The challenge for an actor to play Graham is an interesting one. I am only too aware of the move to be inclusive in casting. Within the small world of my school/youth theatre groups we never had the opportunity to cast someone who was actually blind. Had we have done, I would have jumped at the chance. It would have been preferable.

I am always keen to use appropriate outreach settings to offer relevant experience *(not to mention motivation)*. In this instance it was to play football etc. with Graham or with visually impaired *(young)* people we arranged to meet in the course of our rehearsal period.

However, I am aware the role of Graham *(and Pete etc)* offer a fantastic opportunity for a sighted person to step into the shoes of someone who is visually impaired. You can see, from the accounts of the actors I cast to play this role, how they approached it with a level of commitment to finding their truth and took on all sorts of research. I have never known any role in any of my other plays which led to this level of commitment and experiment.

*

The interesting and insightful part of me doing a 100 metres time-trial blindfolded sprint which ended up with me running into a metal fence was Graham's reaction.

Once he knew I was generally okay he laughed. His laughter showed me, first hand, the challenge of disability does not need to make you a victim. Graham would have laughed his head off if he had done it or any of his mates... blind or otherwise.

Secondly, as Graham pointed out, I learnt more from that experience than any observation. What did he mean?

Did it hurt? Yes.

Did it hurt my pride? Yes, a bit.

Did it stop me wanting to do it again? Of course not. It made me want to do it again but better. Disability can hurt physically and emotionally but it mustn't define you and make you miss out on anything.

People with a disability don't want sympathy; they want a hand to help them up so they can try again.

The extensive research we undertook was a real luxury. I recognised that at the time and, even in a professional context later in life, I never had the chance to research any role so thoroughly.

Matt Allen *(aged 16 when he played Graham in this production in 1984)*

*

I remember the elation of getting the role of Graham but also, and probably more importantly, the feeling of a real responsibility to the subject, especially as at this point I'd not met Graham. I remember when I did meet him I was in awe of him and what he'd achieved. Seeing him and Marie in their own environment, and understanding the total love and understanding they had for each other, their challenges and their successes in life, was fascinating. I count myself very lucky for that opportunity and insight.

I spent hours blindfolded at home. I often recall trying to make a cup of tea and the challenges of that! It's surprising how that engages the way people then understand the challenges the visually impaired have.

Spending time with Graham was invaluable, especially the first time we went for a walk at his local park where he showed me how he could 'hear trees, lamp posts, etc.'! i.e. the bouncing sound-shadows. Hugely important for my performance was understanding the way he looked almost 6 inches above where he believes the sound was coming... and that appears to be the same for many visually impaired people.Then the hand movements and even the differences in his walking.

My whole experience was sealed when Graham said he couldn't have played himself any better... I shall always remember that.

Jason Eames *(aged 16 when he played Graham in this production in 1987)*

*

I remember arriving home and explaining to my mother that I'd been selected to play the lead in Mark's new play. I'll never forget what she said:

'Michael, you're not blind, how the bloody hell are you going to pull that off?'

She doesn't get "acting" and, from that moment on the daunting prospect of developing a blind character would become one hell of a creative endeavour.

There's a line in the play, "Imagine what your knee sees?"

Just think about that.

I needed to draw on holistic experiences. I undertook numerous tasks to help build my understanding of having the sense of sight stripped away. I remember playing with characterisation early on in the process, using big gestures, seemingly always off balance, arms outstretched. I was playing into stereotypical imagery pulled from caricatures or my own imagination. I was wrong in my initial approach and that became apparent rather abruptly when I started wearing a blindfold.

I started with big bold statements of intent, commuting to school blindfolded and spending weekends and evenings blindfolded too.These early experiences were helpful, but ultimately I believe a character is best built through finding nuance: making sandwiches, walking up and down the stairs, washing, going to the toilet, brushing my teeth, tying shoe laces or buttoning a shirt. These smaller tasks presented a unique challenge but, as I overcame them, my confidence grew and those overblown gestures decreased.

I remember how hard we worked. The performances required such focus and energy, and knowing we had to "bring it" every showing was exhilarating.

My family loved it! To this day I have people recalling *Graham* as a piece of theatre they remember. An extended family member was so impressed by the work they saw OYT produce that, when their growing son was old enough, they encouraged him to join a youth theatre, citing OYT as the reason.

Another lad, who I didn't know well, approached me and praised the production and specifically my performance. He informed me that his choice to study theatre and pursue acting came from seeing *Graham*. My mother still insists that *Graham* was by far the best production we'd ever put on.

Michael Mears *(Aged 17 when he played Graham in this production in 2008)*

These notes are taken from Mark's book **Verbatim - The Fun Of Making Theatre Seriously***.*

DVD / Media

There is a DVD of the original award-winning Oaklands Youth Theatre production of this play available.

It is rare that full length productions are made available in this way. It includes a multi-camera-angled professionally filmed version of the play which is ideal to show a class to introduce them to the play.

There is a one-camera-shot version which was shown some months later at the All English Theatre Festival Final *(2008 award winners for ensemble work)*. This will be particularly useful for directors wishing to present this production to analyse as it is in its raw form without any camera trickery!

Media

The media is available for people wishing to present this play. It includes all the original music and media images.

Please contact Salamander Street for further information about the DVD.

Characters

GRAHAM

WORLD'S FASTEST BLIND RUNNER

MARIE

GRAHAM'S WIFE

MAUD

GRAHAM'S MOTHER

HARRY

GRAHAM'S FATHER

JUNIE

GRAHAM'S OLDER SISTER

SUSAN

GRAHAM'S YOUNGER SISTER

MARK

PLAYWRIGHT AND FRIEND OF GRAHAM

ROBERT PHILLIP

SPORTS EDITOR OF SUNDAY TELEGRAPH

CHARLIE

MARK'S SON

NURSE

SISTER BROWN

MR MASON

SENIOR CONSULTANT MOORFIELDS EYE HOSPITAL

MAN

JOHN

CHILDHOOD CONTEMPORARY OF GRAHAM

MADGE

CHILDHOOD FRIEND OF JUNIE

RNIB DOCTOR

CLAUDE

GRAHAM'S UNCLE

TEACHERS 1-5

BILL AITKEN

GRAHAM'S TEACHER

HEADMASTER OF LINDEN LODGE SCHOOL

RE TEACHER

PETE

GRAHAM'S FRIEND (ALSO TOTALLY BLIND)

HEAD TEACHER OF WORCESTER COLLEGE

MR DOWNES

MATHS TEACHER

EMPLOYMENT OFFICERS 1-4

CLIENT

MARION COLLEAGUE AT THE ABBEY NATIONAL

JOGGER

BYSTANDER

WOMAN

RON MURRAY

PROFESSIONAL COACH

ROGER WRAY

GRAHAM'S GUIDE RUNNER IN THE 400 METRES

JOHN ANDERSON

*BRITISH TEAM COACH AND LATER STAR OF TV'S
GLADIATORS*

ANNOUNCER

STARTER

OFFICIAL

SUGGESTED CHARACTER SPLIT FOR SMALLER CAST:

ACTOR 1

MR MASON, GRAHAM

ACTOR 2

MARK, ROBERT PHILLIP, JOHN, CLAUDE,
TEACHER 1, BILL, JOHN ANDERSON,
EMPLOYMENT OFFICER 2

ACTOR 3

CHARLIE, HARRY, TEACHER 2, HEADMASTER,
PETE, EMPLOYMENT OFFICER 4, MATHS
TEACHER, MAN, CLIENT, JOGGER, ROGER

ACTOR 4

MAUD, TEACHER 3, EMPLOYMENT OFFICER 3,
RON MURRAY

ACTOR 5

NURSE, SISTER BROWN, SUSAN, MADGE,
TEACHER 4, HEAD TEACHER WORCESTER
COLLEGE, MARIE

ACTOR 6

ROBERT PHILLIP, JUNIE, RNIB DOCTOR,
TEACHER 5, RE TEACHER, MR DOWNES,
MARION, EMPLOYMENT OFFICER 1,
BYSTANDER, OFFICIAL

This production, that acts as the basis for the post 2008 versions of the script, was first performed by the Oaklands Youth Theatre with the following cast. It won the Adjudicator's Award for ensemble work at the All England Theatre Festival Final in Grays, Essex, June 2008.

CAST LIST

GRAHAM *Michael Mears*

MARIE & ENSEMBLE *Louise Costin*

MARK *Simon Froud*

MAUD & ENSEMBLE *Gemma Priestley*

HARRY & ENSEMBLE *Caidyn White*

JUNIE & ENSEMBLE *Daisy Wheeller*

MR MASON, ANGRY CLIENT, JOHN ANDERSON & ENSEMBLE *Robert Wale*

CLAUDE, MALE DOG, ROGER & ENSEMBLE *Matt Griffiths*

PETE, FEMALE DOG, & ENSEMBLE *Charlie Wheeller*

SISTER BROWN, MARION & ENSEMBLE *Kimberley Cook*

RNIB DOCTOR, RACETRACK OFFICIAL & ENSEMBLE *Kathryn Wiltshire*

BACKSTAGE TEAM

DIRECTORS: *Mark Wheeller & Danny Sturrock*

CHOREOGRAPHY: *Danny Sturrock*

ADVISER TO THE ABOVE: *Callum Dixon*

COSTUME & PROPS: *Kat Chivers*

TECHNICAL DIRECTOR/MULTIMEDIA: *Danny Sturrock*

LIGHTING DESIGN: *Stewart Newton*

LIGHTING & SOUND: *Amy Barnett & Rachael Hampson*

In 2008 during Oaklands Youth Theatre's production of this play, we made a self imposed rule that the only "scene setting materials" were three white chairs and one white stick (walking stick length) per cast member. We used these sticks to create all the environments and shapes we wanted in the production. We adopted this excellent idea from the award-winning Therfield School production which costumed the play in black except for Graham who was in white.

All the actors (except Graham) wore white gloves. The cast intermittently wore simple additional costumes to denote their role or simple hand props painted white e.g. the doctor had a white stethoscope. We dressed Mark in contemporary clothes.

We made a concerted effort to make the production as physical as possible. We used non-speaking cast members wherever possible to help visualise the scenes imaginatively.

Section 1

INTRODUCING GRAHAM

Media 1: Projected onto a screen as the audience enter the auditorium.

"Graham Salmon is the most inspiring athlete I have met; I say this without a moment's hesitation though I have enjoyed the rare privilege of sharing the company of Muhammad Ali, Pele, Sir Gary Sobers, Martina Navratilova, Nadia Comaneci, John McEnroe, Arnold Palmer and countless others in the course of my job." – Robert Philip Sports Editor of the *Daily Telegraph* 1999

*Media 2/Music 1 (**RACE**): A choreographed sequence showing the main aspects of Graham's life. Parents witness him becoming blind as a baby. He goes to school and is expelled. He is happily married. He becomes a world champion runner. He plays golf proficiently. After he strikes the ball, the cast trace the ball with a vocal sound effect and when it lands they cheer and gather round him.*

*Media 3: The video is paused once the image of **GRAHAM** running fades in.*

During the following exchange the cast react to lines which highlight the excitement of the achievement. The pace of the scene should remain fast. The narrated sections should be conveyed more in the style of an excited commentary until the punch in the air.

GRAHAM: *(On the phone.)* Mark! Guess what?

MARK: What?

GRAHAM: Guess!

MARK: You've won the British Open?

GRAHAM: Better!

MARK: Can't be!

GRAHAM: It is! I got a hole in one!

MARK: *(Laughing.)* Seriously? In the British Open?

GRAHAM: Amazing eh?

MARK: At this point I should tell you that my friend Graham Salmon was totally blind… pretty much from birth.

GRAHAM: And I've just been down the bookies and got amazing odds on doing it again.

MARK: *(Laughing.)* Typical!

GRAHAM: I've also got a title for the autobiography I'm working on.

MARK: *(Laughing in expectation.)* Go on…

GRAHAM: Wide Eyed and Legless!

MARK: Mmm…

GRAHAM: You're not keen…

MARK: Let it just sit there eh?

GRAHAM: Well I think it's perfect!

MARK: I'd met Graham in 1983 when I was a young teacher wanting to develop a play with my newly formed Epping Youth Theatre to celebrate the achievements of a local hero. I knew virtually nothing about Graham and he knew absolutely nothing of us… there was nothing to know… we'd only started up a term before. My hard working research group from EYT wrote over over 1,500 sheets of Graham, his family and friends' interview transcripts. We used only the words of these contributors to create the script. We were very strict about this self-imposed rule to make it authentic. The play went on to win accolades at the Edinburgh Fringe and became my first published script… a high point of my career. We developed a wonderful relationship with Graham throughout the long preparation period but all good things come to an end and for our final performance we wanted to do something to mark the occasion.

A group of us went to buy a gift to thank him for the honour of allowing us tell his story. I spotted the perfect gift in a joke shop… but…

ALL: Oh no!

MARK: It was closed. We hammered on the door and when the shopkeeper approached us we explained why we were so desperate. Remarkably, he opened the shop and sold us the item. When we gave this present to Graham, I said: "We've found a very silly present for someone we've learnt can be a very silly man. I'm going to take your glasses away so that there can be no peeping before you open this …" *(Takes **GRAHAM'S** glasses off.)*

GRAHAM: *(Struggling to open the small box.)* I'm not very good at opening presents.

MARK: He opened it and people saw the contents before he did and they laughed. He put his hands inside the box to discover a joke pair of glasses with eyes on springs that come dangling down.

GRAHAM: I creased up! *(Putting the joke glasses on.)* I always brought these glasses out at the end of after-dinner speeches… they always got a great reaction.

MARK: Graham and I went on to develop a lasting friendship and I was proud to have him as my Best Man, and, with his wife Marie, *(Pronounced Mahrie.)*…

MARIE *steps forward to be with* **GRAHAM**.

…they proved wonderful Godparents to our children. *(Laughing.)*

Graham took up golf after retiring from athletics. Most people learn the basics with a friend and then get professional help… not Graham…

GRAHAM: No… get professional help straight away!

MARK: It epitomised his approach. Within a year he was in the British team!

ALL: Wow!

GRAHAM: The year after that, my name was the first on the team sheet!

Everybody laughs gently.

MARK: I used to call him… "Storybook Man". His life was full of exciting achievements…

ALL: *(Punching the air celebratory style.)* Yes!

They bring their arms down chorally in slow motion. Silence.

MARK: *(Changing the pace.)* Unfortunately my "Storybook Man" was equally acquainted with tragedy. Cancer, which caused his blindness as a baby, struck again, just a year after the hole in one.

The chorus form a barrier using their white sticks, between **MARK, GRAHAM** *and* **MARIE**.

GRAHAM: *(Speaking into a telephone with* **MARIE** *emotionally supporting him.)* Mark… I have some very grave news.

MARK: I remember him saying "grave" and thinking that's not a "Graham" word at all.

GRAHAM: They've found a tumour in my thigh… in the muscle…

MARK: What'll happen?

GRAHAM: They have to take my leg away.

MARIE: *(Indicates the line of the amputation on her own body.)* He was to have a hindquarters amputation… a rare and unpleasant operation…

MARK: … but even then Graham found the opportunity to joke.

GRAHAM: With no other blind amputees competing… I'll easily win the American Open!

MARK: He was in hospital for five weeks…

MARIE: I wondered how we'd manage but once he came home, we just got on with it. The hospital staff loved him, and were amazed by his immediate determination to walk.

MARK: And walk he did. He didn't like to use his wheelchair, so often chose to walk even though it hurt. Soon, Marie was telling me about a near miss he had… with his specially designed artificial leg… adapted so he could still play golf!

MARIE: We were at the Golf course practice ground. Graham had got into the buggy and let his artificial leg drop on the floor. It dropped right onto the accelerator.

The cast laugh as the scene is acted out.

He really took off down that hill… at the bottom was a ditch. He knew that but had no idea where the steering wheel was. He had to roll himself out of the damned thing which was still speeding down the hill towards the practice green.

GRAHAM: When Marie got to me I was clutching my stomach…

MARIE: … but he wasn't in any pain.

GRAHAM: I was just pissing myself laughing!

MARK: Things seemed to be improving and then… and then he phoned me following a holiday after the operation. "How was it then?"

GRAHAM: Lovely… yeh…

MARK: Something in his voice told me that was not the full story…

GRAHAM: We had to come home early. My other leg's swollen up.

On MARK's next three lines he attempts to break through the different sections of the (human/white sticks) barrier, running between them for each different line. The barrier becomes ever stronger.

MARK: I didn't know know what to say…

GRAHAM: The cancer's back and they've found nodules in my lungs.

MARK: Can't they do anything?

MARIE: The doctor's told us it's terminal.

In the silence MARK mouths the word "fuck".

GRAHAM: I just want some extra time… with Marie.

MARK: He battled for another year.

MARIE: He was desperate to enjoy Christmas and see in the millennium.

MARK: But that wasn't to be.

MARIE: He was simply too tired to go on. My Graham died in terrible pain in October 1999.

MARK: Graham is the most inspiring person I could ever meet. He represented Great Britain in every major athletics competition between 1977 and 1987. He skied in the Winter Olympics, played cricket at Lords, ran the London Marathon and, for a while, held the British High Jump record for the blind! Robert Philip, Sports Editor of the *Daily Telegraph* summed up Graham's achievements in his tribute saying:

ROBERT PHILLIP: Graham Salmon is the most inspiring athlete I have met. I say this without a moment's hesitation though I have enjoyed the rare privilege of sharing the company of...

ENSEMBLE 1: Muhammad Ali...

ENSEMBLE 2: Pele...

ENSEMBLE 3: Sir Gary Sobers...

ENSEMBLE 4: Martina Navratilova...

ENSEMBLE 5: Nadia Comaneci...

ENSEMBLE 6: John McEnroe...

ROBERT PHILLIP: Arnold Palmer and countless others in the course of my job.

ALL: Graham Salmon is the most inspiring athlete I have met.

Beat.

Media 4: *Slide of* **GRAHAM** *with* **MARIE, OLLIE** *and* **CHARLIE.**

MARK: A few weeks before Graham passed away, my two boys and I visited him at his home. Although I was shocked by how the harsh regime of steroids had transformed his athletic appearance, I was delighted to witness his remarkable spirit was very much alive even in this most difficult period. We were talking when suddenly my six-year-old Charlie said, and bear in mind Graham had just had his leg amputated:

CHARLIE: Will you come out and play football?

MARK: I think his older brother Ollie kicked him but *(Laughing)* to my amusement Graham compiled with Charlie's suggestion and, supported by crutches, swung his good leg at the ball taking shots. My boys were impressed by how many times he scored!

MARIE: As the pain became too much, he sat in his wheelchair and did headers.

Media 5: Pause video once image of **GRAHAM** *running fades in.*

MARK: Graham still wanted to give. Just like in 1983, when he'd given so many hours of his time doing interviews for my first production of *Race*. Ha, I remember before interviewing his mum and dad, they said:

MAUD AND HARRY: No one'll be interested in our story.

MARK: I knew at the time they were wrong… and, now I have the pleasure of inviting you to judge for yourselves…

Section 2

GRAHAM'S EARLY YEARS

Throughout this section, a solo voice hums, then "ah's" then sings an unaccompanied version of "Rock-a-bye-Baby" which underscores the spoken words. The last line of this song should tie in perfectly with the pause before **MR MASON** *says his first line to* **MAUD***. In the original OYT production we had* **BABY GRAHAM** *played by* **GRAHAM***.*

MAUD: Right from when our Graham was born we could see bloodlines through his eyes. Dr Bell at the clinic said:

DR BELL: It's pressure… it'll go in six weeks.

MAUD: He had three nights with thick yellow discharge coming from both eyes.

HARRY: And violent crying.

MAUD: Nothing'd pacify him.

DR BELL: Mrs Salmon! It's only teething!

MAUD: *(To the* **NURSE***.)* When he's in his cot under the light, you can see something white at the back of his eye. Last week I caught my Harry testing his sight with a card. *(To* **HARRY***.)* What are you doing?

HARRY: He can't see out of this eye. *(Referring to his right eye.)*

MAUD: Course he can.

HARRY: He can't… look!

MAUD: He covered up the good eye and put this toy in front of him. Graham never followed it or nothing.

HARRY: Look, if I do it with the other eye; straight away he follows it.

MAUD: Finally they gave me an appointment at Moorfields Eye Hospital.

> **MAUD** *makes her way through a maze of corridors, the outline of which are made by the ensemble with their white sticks.*

MAUD: After two and a half hours being passed from doctor to doctor, I was introduced to Mr. Mason, a senior consultant…

SOLO SINGING VOICE: Down will come baby… cradle and all.

In the OYT production, we had a chorus of voices standing near the scene whispering **MR MASON'S** *words at the same time as* **MR MASON** *to add an intensity to these lines in this and the later section.*

MR MASON: Would you mind if the nurse takes Graham for a moment? I'd like a word with you in private.

MAUD: It was as if he didn't want Graham to hear.

MR MASON: Mrs. Salmon, the white you can see is a tumour. We have to take his eye away. You must bring him in at two o' clock on Monday, next week.

MAUD: I don't know how I got home. It was shattering, just numb. It had been so brutal.

HARRY *enters.*

HARRY: When I got home that lunchtime Maud and Graham weren't there. I didn't think much of it to be honest. I told Junie, our nine year old, that we'd be having sandwiches instead of a proper lunch. Maud returned at about twenty past one. She was crying.

MAUD: They've got to take his eye out.

HARRY: Do what?

MAUD: Take his eye out.

HARRY: What for?

MAUD: He's got a tumour. I wanted you to be there Harry.

HARRY: Can't they do anything else?

MAUD: That's all they told me!

HARRY: I've been telling you for weeks there's something wrong! You told me they said we were "making a fuss".

MAUD: I've been in that hospital for over four hours with Graham crying almost all the time. It's not my fault!

*Music 2 **(Loaded Dice)**: Choreographed sequence showing **MAUD** and* **HARRY** *upset but composing themselves and finally comforting each other.*

MAUD AND HARRY: We've got to get on with it. We've got to take him back there on Monday afternoon.

HARRY: We wanted a photo of him, to remember what he looked like, before… you know… that was very important to us. I booked an appointment at the photographers for that afternoon.

Media 6: Slide of the original photograph.

MAUD: We was a bit disappointed. We couldn't line his eyes up proper but it was a lovely photograph. It was a lovely photograph other than that. That was the only thing we sort of pointed out to one another.

Media 7: Pause video once image of **GRAHAM** *running fades in.*

HARRY: On Monday at 1:30 we arrived at Moorfields and Sister Brown showed us to Graham's room.

SISTER BROWN: Graham will be staying here. You've got nothing to worry about. He'll be thoroughly taken care of.

MAUD: Where am I to sleep?

SISTER BROWN: Didn't Mr Mason explain? The children's ward is in quarantine at the moment with the chicken pox epidemic? I'm afraid you can't stay.

MAUD: I'm still feeding him though.

SISTER BROWN: We'll put him on half bottles, half feeding and gradually wean him off so you can come up at feeding times. Now let me take Graham and we'll see you tomorrow.

MAUD *reluctantly hands* **GRAHAM** *to* **SISTER BROWN**.

MAUD: I felt as if my world had come to an end. I had been promised I could stay.

HARRY: But at 3:30 we had to leave. It was really hard. Sister Brown was marvellous but… but we hated her at the time.

MAUD: I was crying so much you bought me a clock. A smashing little mantle clock, lovely little thing. I remember, I was all red eyed and everybody was staring.

HARRY: *(Laughing.)* They probably thought we'd had an argument.

MAUD: When we went back after, we didn't know what to expect.

HARRY: He had a pad over his right eye and his head was all bandaged up.

MAUD: They'd put cardboard sleeves down his arms to stop him clawing at the bandage. When I picked him up he put his head against my side and started trying to rub it off.

HARRY: We were up there every day for the next three weeks.

MAUD: Nothing else seemed important. It still brings a lump to my throat to talk about it.

HARRY: We told Junie he wasn't exactly the same as he was before.

MAUD: We explained what a dolly looked like when it'd lost an eye and said… "That's what our Graham looks like." She accepted it quite well really.

HARRY: They made Graham an artificial eye.

MAUD: I had to put it in and take it out. It was very unnerving at first but I soon got the hang of it.

JUNIE: Sometimes I had to put Graham's eyes in. To be quite honest I was frightened in case I hurt him. I didn't always put them in the right socket or I put them in upside down. It'd be a bit awkward, I used to get in a bit of a panic but most times I used to get them in all right!

HARRY: They'd found seeds in the other eye so he had ten lots of radium put in over eighteen months.

MAUD AND HARRY: His eye was black and blue and swollen like he'd had a punch up.

MARK: The treatment wasn't working so they offered a new radiotherapy. The problem was it might cause his eye to shrink.

HARRY: We were there for two or three hours, sitting there, waiting.

MAUD: Eventually Mr. Mason came out…

MR MASON: It's not good news.

MAUD: He was almost in tears himself poor man.

MR. MASON: The radium has destroyed the sight in Graham's eye. There is absolutely no hope. The only safe solution is to remove it without delay.

HARRY: What would happen if we were to leave the eye in?

MR MASON: The cancer would penetrate inwards to his brain. He will certainly die. Not only that, but he'll suffer a great deal of pain.

MAUD: Could we give him one of our eyes?

Silence.

MR. MASON: I wish it were as simple as that.We have to have your permission.

MAUD: He'll be blind!

MR. MASON: But he will have a future.

MAUD: That actually wasn't a difficult decision to make.

MR MASON *exits.*

MAUD: The only worry was whether he'd appreciate that we had the opportunity to finish life for him or let him go blind.

HARRY: Were we being selfish keeping him alive?

MAUD: Would all this pain and suffering affect him?

HARRY: Our heads were like bursting with questions:

MAUD: What'll happen when he's an adult?

HARRY: Will he make friends?

MAUD: Will he find a wife, a job?

HARRY: And how will we cope?

MAUD: We'd never met a blind person before…

HARRY: … yet Graham was to be our responsibility.

MAUD: Little did we know how proud we'd become of our Graham.

MARK: Graham has no memory of ever seeing anything… seeing doesn't exist for him. It's like… what does your knee see? Not black… nothing.

GRAHAM: My parents had to discipline themselves to tread the narrow line between protecting me from harm and being overprotective.

MAUD: By the time he was two and a half he knew every inch of Woodland Street where we lived.

HARRY: He could tell every house by its windowsill or door-knocker.

MAUD: I got him to play with his toys on the front doorstep to get other children to mix with him.

Section 3

BEING BLIND AS A CHILD

MARK: I was sent away to Boarding School at the age of nine… those first few months away from my mum and dad proved to be the most distressing period of my life. Graham went as a weekly boarder at the age of four!

HARRY: We got a letter from the RNIB saying:

RNIB DOCTOR: Graham has to have an IQ test so important decisions can be made about his education.

MAUD: *(Proud.)* His IQ was very high. *(Outraged.)* So, they said we should send him to the Sunshine Home for the Blind.

>   **MAUD** *tries to keep hugging* **GRAHAM** *as they, somewhat forcefully remove him from* **MAUD**.

RNIB DOCTOR: You don't want him tied to your apron strings all your life.

RNIB DOCTOR: He needs to be independent.

MAUD: We've always let him be as "independent" as possible.

RNIB DOCTOR: You're not equipped to teach him the things a blind person needs to know in order to be "independent".

MAUD: He's four!

RNIB DOCTOR: He'll be home at weekends.

MAUD: I don't want him to go away!

>   *At this point* **MAUD** *has reluctantly allowed them to remove* **GRAHAM**.

MARK: Despite this Graham was enrolled at the Sunshine Home for the Blind.

HARRY: *(Intimating the long distance from home.)* … in Northwood Middlesex!

GRAHAM: Some of the children there were destructive and I found their behaviour difficult to understand.

JUNIE: Mum and dad were very upset, very upset, sort of, really on thorns all the time. "Is he alright?" and "Would they look after him properly? Keep him clean?"

GRAHAM: I used to look forward to the weekends … I'd come straight home and put my favourite record on.

*Music 3 (**Rock n Rolling**): This rock 'n' roll style track underscores the following scene and stops suddenly when **JUNIE** says, "I hated him!"*

MAUD: Once he got home everyone was waiting… waiting for him to come in!

HARRY: And he'd dance with Junie!

JUNIE: If I didn't he'd pull my hair!

MAUD: Junie!

JUNIE: At the weekends when Graham was home it was all "Graham, Graham, Graham" from Friday evening to Sunday afternoon. I was forgotten! I used to think it wasn't fair. I used to feel neglected. They were so wrapped up in him that there were times when I hated him. I look back and think how silly I was but at the time I hated him.

MAUD: He changed school when he was six and went to North House. A Junior School for blind and partially sighted people.

GRAHAM: I didn't like boarding at all. I'd have rather been at home with Mum and Dad and my sister.

MAUD: North House was a lovely school.

HARRY: He did very well there.

TEACHER 1: Graham Salmon. Aged eight years, ten months. Reading.

TEACHER 2: Is now reading fully contracted Braille.

TEACHER 1: Writing.

TEACHER 2: Steady progress has been made this term. Should aim at more correct work.

TEACHER 1: Speech.

TEACHER 3: *(Loudly.)* Good, but voice production poor.

TEACHER 1: Physical Education.

TEACHER 4: Takes a lively interest in all activities. Making good progress with his swimming.

TEACHER 1: Music: Piano.

TEACHER 5: Should have done very much better if he had applied himself during practice. Inclined to be lazy.

TEACHERS: *(As they exit.)* Inclined to be lazy.

GRAHAM: I never thought I was much different to sighted kids. There were little things like they never ran into lampposts! Nothing was real to me till I touched it. That posed a problem. Not everything I wanted to feel was easily examined by a small boy. One example is something sighted people take for granted, light. I thought the best way for me to experience it was to touch it so Susan took me into our narrow hallway and lined me up under the lampshade on the ceiling. There was little point in me touching it unless it was switched on, so...

SUSAN: I clicked the switch and he was off!

GRAHAM: With one foot on the wall I inched my way up towards the ceiling until I could feel the warmth of the bulb on my face...

SUSAN: ... then, like Columbus landing on America, he touched the "light".

GRAHAM: Owwwww!

SUSAN: The joy of discovery was tempered by pain...

GRAHAM: ... not just from the bulb!

MAUD: His shoes had been muddy.

> **MAUD** *smacks his backside.*

MAUD: My walls were very clean!

GRAHAM: *(Holding his backside.)* So, my path to en "light"enment had to lie low for a few days while Mum cleaned up my quest for illumination!

MAUD: His toys gave him some idea of what things looked like.

GRAHAM: I had loads of soldiers.

Ensemble enter as toy soldiers and adopt suitable poses.

GRAHAM: I could usually find something different about each of them.

As he describes each of the soldiers, he touches them and they make a new, related freeze.

GRAHAM: How they were standing, their guns or the shape of their uniforms. The Arab soldiers were a bit misleading. Their thick robes left me with the impression that all Arabs are extremely fat!

ARABIC SOLDIER: *(Changing freeze to point accusingly at* **GRAHAM**.*)* Oy!

HARRY: He had a stamp book and stamps.

JUNIE: Don't know why? He couldn't have known what the hell they looked like!

MARK: His mum and dad bought him a bike…

MAUD: First… a three-wheeler.

The cast make a trike.

HARRY: Then, when his knees were knocking on the handlebars, we bought him a two-wheeler.

The bike transforms into an exciting looking "monster" two wheeler.

HARRY: He went up and down the street and never went off the kerb.

GRAHAM: *(Proudly.)* One day I ran someone over!

The bike – and **GRAHAM** *– shout at the* **MAN** *making him jump out of the way!*

MAN: Why don't you bloody look where you're going?

GRAHAM: I'm blind! You should get out of my way!!!

MAN: I was so bloody shocked I phoned the bloody newspaper.

GRAHAM: And they took some pictures… of me!

Media 8: Newspaper pictures of **GRAHAM** *on the trike.*

MAUD: I can only remember one time when a sighted kid took advantage of his blindness.

JOHN: Oy ... come here you! Feel this.

GRAHAM: He had this piece of wood and, as I touched it, he placed his hand over mine and pressed it down onto a nail sticking up out of it.

MAUD: The boy's mother was furious!

Media 9: Pause video once the image of **GRAHAM** *running fades in.*

MARK: It's not only children who have the propensity for cruelty. Much later a man bought some second hand Hi-Fi equipment from Graham, real top of the range audiophile stuff. The man paid in tens but told Graham it was twenties.

MAUD: *(Laughing.)* Often Graham would turn it to his advantage. Many's the time we used to think he was asleep, but unbeknown to us...

HARRY:... he was reading his bloody...

MAUD AND HARRY:... braille reading books...

HARRY: ... underneath his sheets. One Friday he told us he wanted a white stick.

MAUD: We got him one.

She hands it to **GRAHAM**.

GRAHAM: Can I go out?

MAUD: Just to the sweet shop.

GRAHAM: Can I have some money?

MAUD: *(Handing* **GRAHAM** *the money.)* Junie!

GRAHAM: Why are you calling her?

MAUD: To look after you.

GRAHAM: I want to go on my own.

MAUD: No!

GRAHAM: Why not?

MAUD: You're not used to it yet! Now, if you want those sweets you'd…

GRAHAM: … alright then!

> **GRAHAM** and **JUNIE** walk off.

MAUD: I went back into the kitchen but was soon joined by Junie, puffing and panting.

JUNIE: Graham wouldn't let me go with him!

MAUD: I had a fit! I went out there and he was nowhere to be seen.

GRAHAM: *(Cheekily.)* I was at the sweet shop!

> *He is being given sweets by the shopkeeper.*

MAUD: They'd given him free sweets and were chatting away to him. After that we let him go out on his own.

MARK: The condemned houses in Woodland Street where the young Graham Salmon lived became a magnificent playground for him and Junie, and on one particular day her friend Madge, to explore…

> *The cast, using the sticks, create a set of obstacles for **GRAHAM** and the two girls to move through.*

JUNIE: We got into this derelict factory by the side of the railway station in Dalston.

MADGE: Go on Graham. I dare you! Climb onto that beam!

GRAHAM: Easy!

MADGE: Go on then.

JUNIE: Show her what you can do Gra!

GRAHAM: I climbed up a pillar and pulled myself onto the beam.

MADGE: He's amazing, your brother is!

GRAHAM: Instinctively, I played up to this encouragement. Now for my tightrope act!

JUNIE: Graham, are you sure?

Everyone breathes heavily.

MADGE: Let him!

GRAHAM: It was narrow and covered with dust which made it seem slippery.

JUNIE: You stay here Madge… I'll go and get Mum…

GRAHAM: Quick Junie!

MADGE: Just stay still! Junie'll be back in a minute.

GRAHAM: I thought I was going to faint!

MAUD: Graham?

GRAHAM: I could barely speak…

MAUD: I wasn't quite so dumbstruck!

GRAHAM: I won't do it again Mum… honest!

MAUD: He didn't.

MARK: But his spirit wasn't dampened.

MAUD: No… not in the slightest!

GRAHAM: From the very beginning, I could sense that I was "special". Being "normal" was never a consideration – I wanted to be the best!

Section 4

A WORLD RECORD

MAUD: When Graham was eleven years old, we moved to Loughton. As our house in Woodland Street was due to be demolished by the GLC.

HARRY: As he was very sports minded, I insisted on moving to a house with a big garden for him to play in.

MAUD: Even so, I used to think to myself 'how is he going to grow up? He's not gonna know anyone.' Occasionally he used to go across to my brother-in-law's house.

CLAUDE: I used to play cricket with him, using a football with lead shot inside which as you can imagine was very hard to bowl. Being blind made no difference to him at all! Quite a few times I'd have to say to him: "We'll have to pack up playing Graham, it's getting too dark."

GRAHAM: Don't worry Uncle. I'll tell you if you hit the wicket!

MAUD: Come on in now Graham, it's getting chilly.

GRAHAM: Oh Mum! One more bowl.

MAUD: Okay, but then you come in.

GRAHAM: Alright.

MARK: It was on one such evening that Claude read an extract to Graham from a book… a big book…

> **CLAUDE** *exaggerates his mime further.*

MARK: The Guinness Book of Records…

CLAUDE: Listen to this Graham.

> *Music 4 **(Impossible Dream?)**: Played quietly underscoring the remainder of this scene.*

GRAHAM: *(Stepping forward to heighten the tension.)* He couldn't have known as he dropped this tit-bit in my ear. He was loading my gun.

GRAHAM *steps forward to create a dramatic moment and place the focus on himself.*

CLAUDE: The fastest time recorded by a blind man running 100 yards is eleven seconds by Geoff Bull.

MARK: *(Contrastingly fast paced.)* Which translates as 12.3 seconds for the 100 metres.

GRAHAM: My target from that moment on was to have my name in that book as the world's fastest blind runner.

CLAUDE: I had no idea he'd set out to do this. He was too busy playing his guitar and wanting to be a rock star.

HARRY: He had already formed a band with some friends at his secondary school and was writing his own songs too!

Section 5

SECONDARY SCHOOL

GRAHAM: Secondary school… hmmm… in 1963, I became a pupil at Linden Lodge School for the Blind. Shortly after I arrived, some younger teachers were appointed with new ideas. One of these was Bill Aitken.

BILL: I came in to a tremendously formal set up.

HEADTEACHER: At Linden Lodge, we provide the normal curriculum of the secondary school with the extra advantage of individual attention possible in classes of not more than twelve. These small classes are an obvious advantage of the special school system.

BILL: The staff there were teachers who "taught".

CLASS ENSEMBLE and **TEACHER** *march in.*

RE TEACHER: *(Announces.)* Religious education. "God punishes people for what they've done."

PETE: Does that mean God's punished me for something by making me blind?

RE TEACHER: Well…

GRAHAM: I was blinded as a baby. How could I've had time to do anything wrong?

RE TEACHER: It could be that God was punishing your parents.

GRAHAM: Are you saying my parents did something wrong?

RE TEACHER: Not necessarily.

GRAHAM: What are you saying? Anyway, if God is supposed to be so good how could he do nasty things like that to people?

RE TEACHER: There's always a reason for everything God does and if someone is blind, there has to be a reason for it.

GRAHAM: Just because someone is blind, or something, it doesn't mean God's punishing them. It's a medical thing. It's nothing to do with religion. That's a load of rubbish!

Enter **HEADTEACHER.**

HEADTEACHER: Silence!

BILL: The priority of the Headteacher, at that time, was academic education and nothing else. Linden Lodge was not preparing kids for the sighted world. We should've been socialising and relaxing then getting ready to do things for themselves.

GRAHAM: I'd been the first person in the school to get a twelve-string guitar. I was so proud of it and my group, the Agreeables…

MARK: … renamed the Disagreeables by his father for obvious reasons.

GRAHAM: *(Laughing.)* …we burst onto the school music scene like the Stones in miniature. One of our gigs was stopped because a group of girls were screaming hysterically at us.

BILL: The Head didn't approve!

HEADTEACHER: Why don't you give up writing stupid songs and dreaming about being a rock star when you should be concentrating on your work?

GRAHAM: We were destined for stardom, so we ignored him!

BILL: They stuck to their guns and even did an audition with Decca!

Music 5: Extract from Decca recording together with slide of the Agreeables.

MARK: Some of his friends were not so complimentary suggesting Graham had…

ALL:… Van Gogh's ear for music!

GRAHAM: This was a very special time; music, friends and sport. What more could a lad want?

MARK: The pop career was somewhat short lived but under the guidance of his inspirational PE teacher, Bill Aitken, Graham began to gain a deeper interest in athletics.

PETE: Up until this point, we had to run with the partially sighted boys in what were called sidecar races.

GRAHAM: We became the partials 'handicap' and got dragged around the 400 metres.

PETE: Bill organised separate races for the totals and the partially sighted.

GRAHAM: We used a running track for the first time instead of just running around on grass.

BILL: I was determined all the totally blind kids should have the sensation of moving at a faster pace rather than just shuffling along. Graham became the first totally blind boy who could provide a challenge to the fastest partials.

GRAHAM: Bill kept encouraging me, and gradually, I got faster.

BILL: In his final term at Linden, Graham felt he could challenge the partials to a race.

GRAHAM: I was really enthusiastic about it and we staged the race at Wimbledon Park.

BILL: Graham won! He was so engrossed in running that I had to shout, "Stop!" I swear, if I hadn't, he would've crashed into the stand. Graham's ability raised my expectations for all the totally blind pupils.

MARK: Bill organised an attempt on the 100 metres world record. He was close…

GRAHAM: … but not close enough.

MARK: There'd be other opportunities. Meanwhile, in his final week of Secondary School, Graham found his (metaphorical) eye had been taken by…

MARK AND GRAHAM: …Marie Pegg… *(Pronounced Mahrie.)*

MARK: … one of the young matrons. His school friend, Pete Young, was determined to get them together…

> **PETE** *enters, making it clear that he too is totally blind. In the original EYT staging, the two boys engaged in an arm wrestle. The victory being scored by* **PETE** *when he gets* **GRAHAM** *to agree to ask* **MARIE** *out.*

PETE: She fancies you.

GRAHAM: How do you know?

PETE: You can tell.

GRAHAM: How?

PETE: She's always faking occasions to meet you.

GRAHAM: Leave it out Pete!

PETE: She's always setting you up as an example…

GRAHAM: You're winding me up!

PETE: … saying how good your posture is.

GRAHAM: Rubbish!

PETE: She fancies you…

GRAHAM: Are you sure?

PETE: Ask her out!

GRAHAM: Pete made me start thinking about her more than I would have done otherwise.

PETE: She thinks you're the King!

GRAHAM: Alright! I'll see what she says.

PETE: Only trying to help mate!

> **PETE** *exits.*

GRAHAM: I knew she'd be going up to change the beds at about 6:45. The sports news came on then so I deliberately left my radio in the dormitory. At twenty to seven, I went up.

> **MARIE** *is making the beds.* **GRAHAM** *bumps into her.*

MARIE: What're you doing here?

GRAHAM: My radio. I've come up to hear the sports news.

MARIE *moves to the other side of* **GRAHAM** *to make another bed.* **GRAHAM** *doesn't notice.*

GRAHAM: I did feel a bit daring. There was a silence for like ages.

MARIE: I didn't help. I was quite shy of fellas.

GRAHAM: In the end I just went ahead and did it.

GRAHAM *facing away from where* **MARIE** *is now making the bed.*

GRAHAM: Actually, I was wondering… if you'd… if you'd like to… you know… come out with me?

MARIE *touches* **GRAHAM** *lightly. He turns round surprised.*

MARIE: "That'll be really nice." *(To audience.)* Pete had told me at breakfast Graham was going to ask me out so I'd already decided.

GRAHAM: Are you free one evening this week or next week maybe when I've left. We could go to the pictures.

MARIE: How about Tuesday? We could go to Hyde Park.

GRAHAM: Yeh… that'd be groovy!

MARIE *goes to* **GRAHAM***. They are about to kiss when* **PETE** *enters.* **GRAHAM** *makes out he's dropped something.*

PETE: Is that you Graham?

GRAHAM: Yeh.

PETE: What're you doing?

GRAHAM: I dropped a book and Marie was up here so I asked her to help me look for it.

PETE: If I leave you two maybe you'll get to feel more than some braille there, Graham.

He laughs then exits.

GRAHAM: That summer with Marie was wonderful.

MARK: The following September Graham started at Worcester College for the blind.

MAUD: Worcester College was reputedly the best school in the world for the Blind.

HARRY: He went there because Linden Lodge were unable to teach Maths to A-Level standard. Graham require this qualification to get onto the RNIB's computer programming course.

GRAHAM: I missed Marie and there was little to enthuse me about sharing the next two years with eighty blind boys.

The males in the cast all cross the stage noisily with white sticks.

I wondered why the education system couldn't allow me, even at six form stage, to attend the local comprehensive. I had one intention to complete my O-level Maths in one year and get out.

GRAHAM *goes to exit.*

HEAD TEACHER: *(Sternly.)* Salmon!

GRAHAM: *(Turning)* The Headmaster had different ideas.

HEADMASTER: You should stay here for two years and while you're here, you must take two A-Levels or we cannot justify having you at the college.

GRAHAM: Still determined to get my Maths and leave, I agreed to do English and History A-Level. Although, I was never really committed to either of these courses.

MARK: Graham's History teacher confirms this in the school report Graham showed me with a wry smile.

MR DOWNES: Grade E. Position in class. Eighth out of eight. Graham has made little effort to reduce his extensive ignorance. I hope, that for his own sake, he will use the amount of ability he undoubtedly has to improve his own general knowledge of the world and cease to rely on other people to do the work for him.

GRAHAM: My Maths was, predictably, a more favourable report.

MATHS TEACHER: He has learnt new work very quickly and performed well on the trial level papers that he attempted. In spite of the rush, I hope he has passed his O-Level.

MARK: What eventually helped Graham to settle was his other love… horse racing. He was always a gambler.

GRAHAM: Not always. *(Grinning.)* I didn't start til I was eleven!

MARK: Graham was soon the driving force behind the racing fraternity at the College!

GRAHAM: But that was only the beginning of the story…

MARK: When we originally developed the play, Graham wrote this song, words and music, describing what happened…

It should be performed as a lively rock 'n' roll number full of shoobedoo's from the ensemble.

GRAHAM: G

> *I was king of the college in my school day*
> G
>
> *I organised the gambling to make it pay*
> D   C
>
> *A turf accountant paid me five per cent commission*
> D   C   G
>
> *And I ran my own book on the chart positions.*
> G
>
> *I'd meet with my friends in the library*
> G
>
> *Study the form and pick a horse or three*
> D   C
>
> *For a year I took bets and avoided detection*
> D   C   G

FRIEND: *He even won money on the general election!*
C   D

GRAHAM: *Until the History teacher came snooping around*
C   D

He caught me laying money with a bookie in town
He said:

        C   G

MR DOWNES: *"At your age, gambling is against the law."*
        D   D7   C D

GRAHAM: *He cancelled the bet and my horse came in at nine to four!*
        G

        I was taken to the Head and was promptly sent home
        G

TEACHERS: *The king of the college was kicked off his throne*
        D   C

GRAHAM: *But the send-off they gave me made the teachers frown*
        D   C D   G

        And the bookies sent the money on, once all the fuss had died down.

GRAHAM: Mr Downes, my History teacher, who was responsible for that damming school report, not only caught me placing the bet but was alone on breakfast duty on the morning of my departure.

MR DOWNES: When it came to the announcements, the cheeky blighter stood up.

GRAHAM: As you will be aware, I'm leaving today. I have one parting thought which I'd like you all to bear in mind.

MR DOWNES: I tried to get him to sit down!

    MR DOWNES *makes his way to* **GRAHAM**.

GRAHAM: Remember my friends…

MR DOWNES: Sit down boy… sit down!

MR DOWNES *tries to make* **GRAHAM** *sit down.*

GRAHAM: Radix malum est cupidas.

MARK: Roughly translates as "money is the root of all evil".

MR DOWNES: *(To* **MARK**.*)* You can shut up too!

GRAHAM: Mr Downes was not amused… and as I sat down the entire dining room erupted into a rousing chorus of *"For He's a Jolly Good Fellow"* accompanied by clapping, stamping and lots of banging on tables. One of the kitchen maids came out of the kitchen and kissed me goodbye, wishing me luck. She said they'd all miss me!

HARRY: The headmaster…

MARK: … who was also a Justice of the Peace…

HARRY: … rang up to tell us Graham was to be sent home.

MAUD: Twelve of them got suspended. He used to take bets from some of the teachers, but of course, he couldn't say anything or he'd get them into trouble.

HARRY: I wasn't bothered because he'd already decided to leave in a couple of weeks anyway and he'd already taken his O-level Maths.

JUNIE: That's not what I remember! You were absolutely disgusted! I can't remember exactly everything but you said… "The little sod! I'll have a go at him when he gets home." Don't you remember?

HARRY: I could hardly let on to a JP that I knew all about it!

JUNIE: No Dad! You'd bought him this expensive blue trunk for all his gear to go in. You were saying: "All that bloody money we've spent out and he's not been there long!"

MARK: And what was Graham's reaction? Ashamed? Worried? Concerned?

GRAHAM: No way!!! *(Laughing.)* I was delighted to have an extra fortnight's holiday!

When linking this section with the next, the cast circle around – as though on dodgem cars – perhaps accompanied by fairground music.

Section 6

UNEMPLOYMENT – EMPLOYMENT

MARK: Sometimes Graham made his blindness appear as a bonus, an additional ability. Ordinary events became extraordinary. Dodgem cars were one example. His driving was, you could say, a sight for sore eyes. The attendants, with a smile, allowed him to contravene the "one way only" rule!!! But how did he feel inside? Was he always positive? He was asked in a TV interview if he was ever bitter about being blind. Initially, he said no but when the interviewer probed he said…

GRAHAM: Actually I was once. I'd qualified to be a computer programmer but no one'd employ me. It was as if I would never get a job, never have any money and independence.

MARK: Our attitudes and laws have changed in the intervening years but remember, everything you hear in this scene was actually said to Graham.

MAUD: He typed out over sixty application letters and got four replies.

*Media 10/Music 5 **(Prejudice)**: Personnel Officers relating to **GRAHAM** animating their prejudicial views towards him. The lines crescendo to a shout, whereupon **GRAHAM** slams the phone down. A note to directors is that you should avoid the PO's merely encircling **GRAHAM** and falling on the floor at the height of the crescendo!*

ALL: Don't worry Mr Salmon. We will call you back.

PO 1: It could be a bit difficult.

PO 2: You wouldn't be able to manage.

PO 3: We don't employ blind people.

ALL: Don't worry Mr Salmon. We will call you back.

Media 11: Pause video once the image of Graham running fades in.

GRAHAM: People would be interested then I'd say "I'm blind"…

Shouting at **PO 4** *as the lift door opens (indicated by the arms of the* **PO***'s) and pushing him out of the way.*

PO 1: Oh. Oh dear.

ALL PO'S: Oh dear!

PO 1: That could be a bit difficult.

GRAHAM: Why?

In the 2008 OYT production, **THE PO'S** *formed a huddle upstage competing not to talk to* **GRAHAM,** *then, one by one are pushed forward to present (mock-proudly) their pathetic and patronising excuses.*

PO 2: Erm… well… the office entrance is down a small side turning. Lorries often come and go.

PO 3: A blind person would be a severe drain on our sophisticated system.

PO 1: The staff aren't very thoughtful…

PO 2: … the toilet seats are sometimes dirty.

PO 3: We make tea for meetings… take it in turns… with a very hot kettle!

PO 1 – 3: You wouldn't cope.

PO 3: We can't employ blind people. It's a pity, we'd like to help.

PO 4: We're on the sixth floor. You won't be able to manage the stairs.

GRAHAM: What's wrong with them?

PO 4: They're… they're awkward… we're on the sixth floor.

GRAHAM: I'm blind… I have no problem with stairs!

Silence.

PO 4: I'll take your number and call you back.

They replace their respective receivers.

GRAHAM: Montague Evans did phone back and gave me the break I was looking for. Ironically the job was on the third floor and…

All **PO'S** *and* **GRAHAM** *present as a group of people in a lift.* **PO 4** *moves towards them pressing the lift call button saying:*

PO 4: "Ding".

Shouting at **PO 4** *as the lift door opens and pushing him out of the way. It is indicated by the arms of the* **PO'S**.

ALL: There was a lift!

GRAHAM: Just before I started at that job, one of the most chilling episodes of my life occurred. It was a particularly quiet afternoon and no one was within earshot, when I suddenly heard the tyres of a car screech and a loud thud.

A choreographed sequence. In the 2008 OYT production, this was staged with the cast staging a (two) horse race with ensemble improvising a commentary behind them. The horse and rider morph into a car and the scene builds to a hit and run car accident. A child is the victim. A mother is left with her child who has been knocked over.

GRAHAM: The car accelerated again. It was about 200 yards away. It was not difficult to put two and two together. A hit and run accident and I was the only witness. What should I do? Run into the road, stand in the car's path and hold up my stick? What if the car doesn't stop? I couldn't do that? I might be wrong.

Could I pick something up to throw at the car to force it to stop? Again, there was nothing to throw. Should I call for help? That too was useless, there was nobody about. The car flashed by and I continued on my way. As I approached the point where I'd heard the accident, a crowd of people were gathering around.

WOMAN/BYSTANDER: *(To* **GRAHAM**.*)* Has someone called an ambulance?

GRAHAM: A woman was sitting crying. It was her son. He was only ten and they were not too sure how badly he was hurt. He wasn't crying so I guessed he was unconscious.

WOMAN/BYSTANDER: I think his arm's broken. *(To* **GRAHAM**.*)* Oy mate, did you see anything?

GRAHAM: I felt so useless.

ALL: Oy mate... did you see anything?

GRAHAM: Then they must have seen my stick. I was the only witness and all I could tell them was which direction the car took at the crossroads. As I walked by, I wondered if I should say anything more but what could I say? I carried on. That memory has haunted me ever since.

Beat.

MARK: Graham had a successful career, twenty-five years which were at the Abbey National. Most customers didn't realise he was blind... but there was always the exception...

CLIENT: I have a query on my income tax and I'd like some advice.

GRAHAM: Can I look at your passbook?

CLIENT: Of course.

GRAHAM: I won't keep you a minute.

   GRAHAM *goes to exit.*

CLIENT: Can't you read them here? Is something wrong with your eyes?

GRAHAM: Yes... I'm blind.

CLIENT: Then get the manager.

GRAHAM: He's out.

CLIENT: I don't want you taking my books away. I'll see his deputy!

GRAHAM: I only need them for a minute.

CLIENT: I'm not unsympathetic. I just want to be served by someone who can see.

GRAHAM: I wanted to tell him it's people like him who stop people like me getting jobs and when we get one, stop us from getting on. I wanted to have a go at him but I came in and asked Marion, our principal clerk, to see him.

MARION: On his way out he had the cheek to say.

CLIENT: How generous of the company to give someone like him a job!

MARION: We couldn't do without him!

MARK: Customers like that were few and far between…

GRAHAM: … my time at the Abbey was very important to me.

MARK: The Abbey National gave Graham respect and recognition of his ability, not his disability. He was there because he was an asset to the company. By the end of his career, he was the number one Financial Advisor in the City. He was also very popular in his office and his colleagues all had stories about him…

*Music 6 **(Mission Urinal)**: Boys position themselves as though hidden in toilets for next story!*

MARION: Some lads put a toilet brush upside down in the urinal with the bristly bits sticking out. When it touched his willy, he thought it was a rat and jumped back in horror.

GRAHAM: The funny thing was that the guys who perpetrated that joke hid behind the door… and switched off the light…

The boys in the toilets gradually stop laughing as they realise what they have done!

… so that I… so that I couldn't see them!!!

The boys are silent momentarily then call each other idiots and skulk off stage annoyed.

MARK: So back in 1973, with his first job and money, Graham began to see his friends from school again. They formed a sports club for the blind.

MARIE: That same year Graham and I married.

HARRY: It takes a special kind of person to become attached to someone in Graham's position.

MAUD: Marie is a very special person. Graham thought the world of her and she of him. It was a match in a million.

MARK: Now… *(Walking into the audience… the house lights come up.)* I know this breaks the conventions of a play, halting its progress and all that but… this play doesn't do Marie justice. Nearly all the words in this script are taken from interviews with people involved in Graham's life and Marie didn't like interviews. So, it falls to me to say my piece.

Marie enabled Graham to enjoy the success he achieved. She was never sidelined and she played an important part of the management side of the British Blind Athletics team. She was a devoted wife and, in his final months, an incomparable carer. I remember, at Graham's funeral, the priest said: "We are passing Graham's body into the care of God." … and quite spontaneously I whispered to my wife: "God's got a hell of a job to live up to the care Marie had given him." Marie lives to give. In his final months, Graham wrote a number of songs and recorded them in his home recording studio. One was called simply… *My Wife*. I hope Graham's version of this very personal song goes some way towards redressing the balance.

*Media 12 / Music 7 (**My Wife by Graham Salmon**):*

SONG 4: My Wife
by Graham Salmon (1999)
Words & Music by Graham Salmon

GRAHAM:

Eb Bb Cmin7

   Fmin   *Bb*
I have climbed many mountains, reached many goals

   Fmin   *Eb*
And she's always been there beside me

 Fmin   *Bb*
She reaches out her hand and she touches my soul

   Fmin   *Eb*
And she gives all her love to guide me.

Ab   *Eb*
Always there behind the scenes

Ab   *Bb*
Never wanting the glory

Ab   *Eb*
Hope she knows how much she means…

Ab   *Bb*
Without her there's no story

Eb Bb   Cmin
Oh life… life is my wife

Fmin   Bb
We have laughed in the sunshine and we've cried in the rain

Fmin   Eb
And we've been through it all together

Fmin   Bb
With a smile on our faces we can beat any pain

Fmin   Eb
And we'll hold on to each other forever.

ALL:

Ab   Eb
Always there behind the scenes

Ab   Bb
Never wanting the glory

Ab   Eb
Hope she knows how much she means…

Ab   Bb
Without her there's no story

Eb Bb   Cmin
Oh life… life is my wife.

> *Media 13: Pause video once the image of Graham running fades in. Cast form a straight line as though to dive into a pool.*

MARK: Graham's Metro Sports and Social Club was accorded charity status.

MARIE: He involved himself in the fund raising, participating in, amongst other things, a sponsored swim.

MARK: Graham's swimming bore little relation to his fishy surname. Doggy Paddle was Graham's aquatic party piece!

All dive in and swim across an easy "length" with **GRAHAM** *quickly falling behind. As* **MARIE** *speaks,* **GRAHAM** *does a frantic but less effective doggy paddle mime!*

MARIE: Even so, no one could talk him into doing any less than the others.

All except **GRAHAM** *are now at the other side of the pool, cheering* **GRAHAM** *on.*

MARK: His companions describe how they waited around for what seemed like weeks while he completed his thirty lengths!

They continue to shout encouragement to **GRAHAM** *who is doing his comic doggy paddle stroke. He approaches the side of the pool… at one point moving backwards… where they wait for him. In slow motion he puts out his hand to touch the edge and says:*

GRAHAM: One!

The cast groan in anti-climax.

Section 7

RACE TO BE SEEN – EPPING YOUTH THEATRE

MARK: A few years later I arrive in the story, nervously dialling Graham's phone number, planning to reveal my big idea of writing a play telling the story of his life… *(GRAHAM picks up the phone receiver.)* and all I'd been told was that he was blind and that he "did some running".

GRAHAM: It sounds interesting but I'm… well, I'm very busy because I'm training for the European Championships in Bulgaria.

MARK: Wow! I had no idea! I don't expect you to commit here and now but I'd like to meet if that's possible.

GRAHAM: My ego took over and we fixed a meeting for the next week.

MARK: I was so excited but what would he think to us, an inexperienced youth theatre group.

GRAHAM: I was grinning broadly as I told Marie of Mark's plans.

MARIE: *(To GRAHAM.)* A play?

GRAHAM: Yeh.

MARIE: *(Joking.)* I hope you told him where to go!

GRAHAM: It'll probably come to nothing.

MARIE: I don't want people delving into our private life.

GRAHAM: If you don't want him to come, I can ring and tell him not to.

MARIE: You got his phone number?

GRAHAM: I'm sure I can get it… somehow…

MARIE: The problem is…

GRAHAM: What?

MARIE: The problem is Graham Salmon… if something does come of it, I know you'll love it!

GRAHAM: So, that's a yes then?

When Mark was late, I wondered if he was a crank having a joke at my expense.

MARK: *(Now wearing a motorbike coat and carrying a motorbike helmet.)* The truth was I'd got lost! I was three quarters of an hour late and really annoyed with myself and *(Someone hurls a cup of water over* **MARK**.*)* …it was pouring with rain!

And I was on a motorbike!

MARIE: He looked like something from outer space!

GRAHAM *and* **MARK** *shake hands.*

GRAHAM: Something very wet from outer-space!

MARK: Graham introduced me to his life and talked about his athletics.

GRAHAM: Things had been so amateurish.

MARIE: At the Stoke Mandeville Games you'd caused such a sensation…

GRAHAM: They made us have a guide runner in the 100 metres.

MARIE: Graham's was holding him back!

GRAHAM: So I let go and won!

MARIE: But he was disqualified and put in…

GRAHAM AND MARIE: … third place.

MARIE: Where the guide had come!

GRAHAM: The next year we were "allowed to" run alone with a caller but the PA was blasting out so loud, we couldn't hear anything! It was like a school sports day.

MARIE: We wanted real sport not "specially adapted games".

GRAHAM: *(Laughing.)* In the 800 metres we actually had a man at the end of the first lap saying…

MARIE AND GRAHAM: Ding-a ling! *(Laugh.)*

GRAHAM: Cos they didn't even have a bell to ring!

MARIE: If you dared suggest they get a starter they'd say.

GRAHAM: Do you think these people will give up their time to come and shoot the gun for you!!!?

MARIE: The organisers didn't understand.

GRAHAM: So we set Metro up and showed Stoke Mandeville how it should be done! I contacted Ron Murray, a professional coach.

RON enters.

RON: *(Introducing himself in a military manner.)* Hello… Ron Murray.

GRAHAM: He'd coached Barbara Inkpen to a silver medal at the Munich Olympics. *(To RON on the phone.)* I think I should tell you… I'm blind.

RON: Why do you want to do the high jump?

GRAHAM: I want to break the world record.

RON: Good for you! I've actually helped blind people before.

GRAHAM: He'd been an officer in the Royal Navy and sounded like one as he barked out his instructions.

RON: Have to take a look at you! Monday evening. Six o' clock. Restaurant. Crystal Palace!

GRAHAM: He taught me the Fosbury Flop.

MARK: I saw Graham doing this successfully but also misjudging the moment when he should jump, landing across the bar, or missing the protected landing area altogether. There were never any words of complaint. He just got up to try again! He went on to set the British record.

GRAHAM: 1 metre 38…

MARIE: 4 feet 7 in old money.

MARK: *(To audience.)* About neck height to an average adult.

GRAHAM: One training session, Ron was watching me run and suggested I take up sprinting.

RON: And soon it was better than his high jump. He ran the 100 metres in 12.6 seconds and became the first blind person to run in public against sighted athletes. The British record which stood at 12.5 seconds was a real possibility.

GRAHAM: It frustrates me to have to rely on others for help. I wanted to train every night but knew no one who'd fit in with these plans.

MARIE: He still practised nightly.

GRAHAM: Marie would call me from the top of this steep hill to test my strength and stamina.

MARIE: We were knackered with the effort of it all but I wouldn't have it any different and he went on to break the 100 metres world record.

MARK: What?

GRAHAM: Yeh. Three days before my twenty-sixth birthday.

MARK: What was your time?

GRAHAM: 11.4 seconds…

MARK: Not that different to the sighted record!

GRAHAM: Then I won the *Daily Mail* Athlete of the Month Award.

MARIE: Alan Wells was the runner up.

GRAHAM: *(Laughing.)* I beat an Olympic champion! It was fantastic to fulfil my childhood dream!

MARIE: The RNIB, seeing what Graham had achieved, set up a national coaching scheme for blind athletes using top national coaches. He was really making an impression!

MARK: How do you… how do you actually do the hundred metres without a guide?

Media 14: Footage showing **GRAHAM** *doing the 100m.* **GRAHAM** *making bathroom furniture and a football match for the blind.*

GRAHAM: Two callers stand on the track, one at 30 metres…

MARIE: Usually me…

GRAHAM: **…** yeh so Marie's voice is clear as I leave the blocks. The other stands beyond the finish…

MARIE:… takes over once Graham is past 30 metres.

GRAHAM: They call continuously using a number system.

MARIE: Five, the centre track number, means he's straight. If the number gets lower he'd know that he's running towards the inside of the track … likewise higher… towards the outside.

GRAHAM: If I hear the caller calling out "One", I know I'm about to be speared by a javelin! *(They laugh.)* I didn't just want to be a good athlete. I wanted to look like a good athlete.

MARIE: We showed Mark a video showing Graham using a circular saw and an electric drill.

MARK: I had to remind myself he was totally blind. I could never make bathroom furniture!

GRAHAM: *(Grinning.)* I showed him a football match for the blind.

MARK: They used a ball with lead pellets in it so that they can hear it. I had a great evening. We really clicked. I loved his sense of humour!

GRAHAM: As an Arsenal fan I've sometimes found it a blessing to be blind!

MARK: He was full of funny stories…

Media 15: Pause video once the image of **GRAHAM** *running fades in. The cast reposition themselves for this story. Humour can be enhanced by humans playing the dogs!!!*

GRAHAM: I had a rather unusual experience with our family pet Jack Russell, Ringer. I was talking him for a walk in Pyrles Lane, a road in Loughton, as was my custom whilst I was out of work. Ha ha. I was the only one who could get the dog to walk straight as he had a tendency to run off in any direction. However, he stopped as most dogs do when nature calls. We were passing an open field. This was a little unusual as he normally chose the bushes. He seemed to be taking rather a long time. I tugged at the lead but he wouldn't budge. I waited a little longer and tried again. One or two other dogs started to arrive and were standing around growling. I was beginning to worry about what might happen. Would they attack him? Would there be one hell of a fight with me caught up in the middle of it? Strangely though, none made any move to come closer. I tugged again at the lead but still no response.

Enter **JOGGER**.

JOGGER: "You won't move him for a little while friend!"

    JOGGER *exits, smiling.*

GRAHAM: As he ran off, I wondered what he meant so I ran my hand down the lead only to find Ringer right on top of a bitch. They say dogs are a man's best friend. On this occasion the roles were reversed. I put myself in his shoes and just stood there, waiting while he… while he indulged himself!

MARK: We could write a play about Graham but how would we fit everything in?

    Media 16: Footage of the original EYT production.

GRAHAM: I was impressed by their energy and particularly the idea that the script would use the words spoken in interviews.

MARK: That was important to me… I wanted it to be as authentic as possible.

GRAHAM: The effort they put into writing that script was comparable to that of a successful athlete.

MARIE: We attended almost every performance and remember our time with EYT, and later OYT, very fondly.

    Media 17: Pause video once the image of **GRAHAM** *running fades in.*

    Beat.

MARK: I decided the final scene of *Race* would end with what happened at the European Championships in Bulgaria, due a month or so before our premiere!

GRAHAM: My first international gold medal would make a brilliant ending!

MARIE: Although he entered for the 100 meters, his major hope rested on the 400.

    Media 18: Footage in slow motion of **GRAHAM** *and* **ROGER** *running the 400 metres is shown. Pause video once the image of* **GRAHAM** *running fades in.*

MARK: Graham ran the 400 metres with a guide runner attached to him by a short length of rope.

ROGER *enters.*

GRAHAM: I had a brilliant relationship with Roger Wray, a top athlete from my club, Haringey. He generously sacrificed his own career to train with me and help achieve my goals.

MARK: A gold medal would make a perfect ending for us. It seemed "meant to be".

ROGER: Graham got into the shape of his life and me along with him.

GRAHAM: Everyone says I'll get gold in the 400 and bronze in the 100. I reckon I'll get gold in both!!!

MARK: In those days it wasn't televised so I phoned his mum after each race. First came news of the 100.

MAUD: It's not good Mark.

MARK: What happened?

MAUD: Ninth.

MARK: Ninth? How's Graham about it?

MAUD: He's worried about the play...

MARK: Tell him not to be.

MAUD: That's not all. A Russian broke his world record. 11.38. He's not too bothered about that but he was gutted at coming ninth!

MARK: Wish him luck for the 400. I replaced the receiver. I hadn't ever considered what'd do if he didn't give us the dream ending! I realised an anti-climactic ending might not work. What should we do? The next day I was back on the phone.

MAUD: *(Excitedly screeching the good news.)* He's through to the final of the 400's.

MARK: *(Not looking at **MAUD** to maintain the illusion of being on the phone, pokes his ear to show how loud her voice is on the phone.)* Brilliant!

MAUD: 56.2. He wants to break the world record.

MARK: *(To audience.)* The 400m world record for a Blind person then stood at 55.8. But what about the opposition? Graham had told me before he left.

GRAHAM: Franck of Germany… his best time is 56.5 but he was absolutely knackered after. In the same race I did 56.6 but I had lots left. I can beat him, I know I can!

MARK: In that same recorded interview, I asked him why he raced. His answer was instant.

GRAHAM: I enjoy trying to win, that's what motivates me. People reckon I'm trying to prove something because I'm blind. That's rubbish! If I didn't enjoy it I'd never do it.

MARK: Obviously I know the result but maybe you don't so cut to the final scene Graham created for us in 1983 at the European Championship B1 400 metres Final.

Media 19: Pause video once the image of Graham running fades in.

GRAHAM: I felt so tired after the heats and ached everywhere.

MARIE: John Anderson, the British team manager…

MARK: … later host of the TV show *Gladiators*…

MARIE: … told Graham…

JOHN: You were the best prepared, physically and mentally. Your team work with Roger was by far the most polished.

MARIE: As we went up to bed he warned.

JOHN: The worst thing you can do is run the final in your mind.

GRAHAM: Before going to sleep, I put a Beatles cassette on. I remember thinking they were the masters of music and tomorrow I will prove I'm master of the track.

The cast could sing the "Boy, you're gonna carry that weight… a long time." under these lines, segueing into the nightmare sequence.

GRAHAM: I slept solidly until about 2:30, when I woke up, thinking about how I'd start the race. My sleep was fitful after that.

A nightmare is staged featuring **GRAHAM'S** *anxiety about the final, accompanied by a cacophony of voices and attempting to hold him back or disrupt his focus. The use of lighting and slow motion serves to make this more threatening.*

ROGER: Breakfast was at seven.

GRAHAM: I couldn't eat a great deal.

MARIE: We arrived on the track at about eight o' clock.

ROGER: The sun was blazing down on Varna Stadium.

The chorus make sizzling sounds and point their sticks at **GRAHAM** *and* **ROGER**, *representing the heat rays of the sun.*

MARIE: Graham and Roger climbed to the back of the stands to find shade.

The chorus stop sizzling/pointing and say ahhh!

JOHN: In 90 minutes Graham would know if all their hard work would be rewarded.

GRAHAM: My legs still felt sore from the previous evening's heats.

MARIE: He stretched out on a bench and tried to relax.

ROGER: We could hear flags flapping in the wind and a buzz of conversation among the competitors and spectators.

MARK: Thoughts flooded into Graham's mind with no rhyme nor reason.

MAUD: Unconnected incidents like how as a child he had ridden his bike so independently in Woodland Street.

MARIE: How, in his youth, he'd dreamed of finding fame…

GRAHAM:… and fortune…

MARIE:… as a rock star.

HARRY: How he became the hero at Worcester College, getting himself thrown out for running bets.

JOHN: His meeting with Ron Murray and the night he became the first blind athlete to compete on equal terms with sighted athletes.

ALL: His 100 metres world record!

ROGER: We talked about friends at home…

MARK: Mark and the Epping Youth Theatre waiting eagerly for the results of the race before completing their play!

MAUD: His mum…

HARRY:… and dad…

MAUD: …waiting…

HARRY: … anxiously…

MAUD AND HARRY:… nervous but very proud.

MARK: He wondered where Marie was…

MARIE: Marie, who worked so hard and sacrificed so much for his success…

MAUD:… who always had the right words when things went wrong…

HARRY AND MAUD:… who was so completely dedicated.

HARRY: He knew how much a gold medal would mean to her.

ALL: He had to win.

MARK: They started the long descent of the steps to the track and walked to the car park to begin their warm up.

GRAHAM: My legs felt tired.

MARIE: That was worrying.

ROGER: We listened for the announcement to bring us to the track.

GRAHAM: I recalled the words of Betty Hill, widow of the world champion racing driver…

MARIE: "It takes sheer guts and courage to run when you're blind, let alone sprint like that. I compare it to my Graham getting into his racing car when he couldn't walk."

ANNOUNCER: *(FX or through megaphone.)* Athletes for the men's B1 Men's 400 metres final, report to the start immediately.

GRAHAM: We were drawn in lanes seven and eight.

MARK: Roger, unlike the other guides, ran on the outside of the blind competitor.

MARIE: I went to cheer him from the 200 metres mark and looked back. Something was going on between Graham, Roger and an official.

ROGER: I run this side.

OFFICIAL: *(To* **ROGER** *in broken English.)* Him other side!

ROGER: I run this side!

OFFICIAL: Him other seiter unt lane eight marker.

ROGER: *(Calmly.)* No… we stay here.

OFFICIAL: Uzzer seiter!

MARIE: Then John Anderson the British Team coach got involved.

JOHN: What's going on?

ROGER: They want me to run on the other side.

JOHN: He can't! They've trained this way round.

OFFICIAL: The others. They do!

JOHN: They run like this so they start in lane seven!

OFFICIAL: Lane eight!

JOHN: I'll make an official protest!

JOHN: You cannot do this to athletes before a race!

OFFICIAL: *(Walking off.)* I make report…

ROGER: John. Leave it! We've got what we wanted. We can sort it out after.

*Music 8 (**Ona Strt**): (FX)*

STARTER: Ona strt!

GRAHAM: Roger, who'd been talking to John, was now facing the wrong way!

ROGER turns and makes as if starting the race from a standing position.

ROGER: Graham…forward a bit…

JOHN: *(Running behind* **GRAHAM** *and* **ROGER.***)* Stop the race! Official protest!

*Music 9 **(Gotozi)**: (FX)*

STARTER: Gotozi

JOHN: Protest!

GRAHAM: For a split second, it flashed through my mind. Should I stand up? Should I support John's protest?

JOHN: Stop the race!

GRAHAM: Instantly I told myself… don't be a fool…

A starting pistol fires.

ALL: Run!!!

MARIE: Come on Gra!

*Music 10 **(Starting Pistol)**: **MARIE** and **JOHN** shout encouragement to **GRAHAM**.*

*Music 11 **(Race To Be Seen)**: There are innumerable ways of staging this race. However, the guiding principals will be the same. The director/cast should aim to communicate the achievement, excitement and energy/effort expounded. I will explain how I came to direct what I consider to be the most successful staging with Oaklands Youth Theatre in 2008. This is offered by way of help rather than prescription. I was keen to get the audience puffing and panting with the runners. They need to "feel" the effort. Thus, I presented them with cast members actually tiring themselves out on stage.*

GRAHAM *and* **ROGER** *are in freeze frame as though running together throughout the first 45 seconds of the "race". They make single steps forward every ten seconds. Beside them, in pairs, eight members of the cast run from the back of the stage to the front, bend, touch the floor, turn then from the front to the back, bend to touch the floor and so on, each "run" taking approx one second. Each pair begins according to who is the fittest. The* *fittest goes first and finishes last. The second pair start running on 8, the third on 12 and the fourth on 18. The whole cast count chorally from 1 – 55, representing the number of seconds it took Graham to run this race with* **MARIE** *and* **JOHN** *shouting encouraging words in support of* **GRAHAM**. *Gradually the runners drop out. The first to drop out on 38, the second on 44 and the third on 50.*

As soon as they stop running they breathe heavily to show the effort as though they are trying to re-gain their breath/composure. At 50, **GRAHAM** *and* **ROGER** *start running on the spot in slow motion. The others watch in slow motion. When they get to 55 everyone cheers.* **GRAHAM** *and* **ROGER** *adopt a victory pose with linked hands held aloft. All crowd around congratulating them.* **MARIE** *makes her way to* **GRAHAM** *and* **ROGER** *as the cheering dies away and the crowd move back.*

MARIE: What happened Gra? Did you win?

Silence.

GRAHAM: Course I did!

MARIE: *(Hugging* **GRAHAM**.*)* I couldn't see! Amazing!

Silence. The cast re-group.

GRAHAM: I didn't catch my time when it was announced. I was so wrapped up in the celebrations. Everyone was slapping me on the back, shaking my hand, offering me drinks but I started to wonder what my time was. I had one hell of a shock when they told me! "What?"

ALL *(EXCEPT* **GRAHAM**.*):* Fifty-five point five!

GRAHAM: Yes!

MARIE: A new world record!

The action freezes.

JOHN: The era of Britain winning gold medals in these games began with Graham Salmon in Bulgaria. He's an inspiration to everyone. Britain should be proud of him.

MARK: Back at home, we were celebrating too! The dream ending from my Storybook Man!

*Music 12 **(Medal Ceremony)**: The following lines play with echo effects up to* **GRAHAM**'s *line "Mark, I have some very grave news".*

ANNOUNCER: The medal ceremony for the B1 Men's 400 metres.

*   **GRAHAM** *steps up on a podium to receive his medal.*

VOICE 1: Were we being selfish keeping him alive?

VOICE 2: I'm not unsympathetic, I just want to be served by someone who can see…

VOICE 3: A blind person would be a severe drain on our sophisticated system…

VOICE 4: I'm afraid we don't employ blind people…

VOICE 5: You won't be able to manage the stairs.

As this is said **GRAHAM** *bows his head to have* **JOHN ANDERSON** *place around* **GRAHAM'S** *neck… a gold medal.*

ANNOUNCER: And in first place, Graham Salmon of Great Britain, in a new world record time of 55.5 seconds.

GRAHAM FX: *(***GRAHAM** *adopts a victory salute on his podium.)* Mark, I have some very grave news…

Silence. The cast gently sit on the stage looking towards **MARK**.

MARK: I'd like to end this performance by asking you to listen to an out-take of the final radio interview the real Graham did for Radio 4's *In Touch*. It was about his determination to continue playing golf with his false leg. It'll leave you with a sound I remember as being so much a part of Graham… laughter.

The lights dim to black and the outtake is played.

*Music 13 **(In Touch Out-take)**: The cast stand and bow. As the audience leave the picture of* **GRAHAM** *remains on the screen.*

*Music 14 **(Race To Be Seen by Graham Salmon / Mark Wheeller)**: The original Race To Be Seen song sung by Bernadette Chapman from Epping Youth Theatre is played as the audience leave.*

The title Song of the Play
SONG 1: RACE TO BE SEEN (1983)
Words by Graham Salmon
Music by Mark Wheeller

INTRO:

E9   E   Emaj7   E6   B/E   A/E   E

E9   E   Emaj7 E6   B/E A/E   E
There's a race at the national stadi-um... all tickets have been sold.

E9   E   Emaj7 E6   A/B   Amin/B E
The world's top runners will be there... trying to take the gold.

D/E   E9 D/E   E
Their determination each to win mean that...

D/E   E C/E D/E E9 E Emaj7 E6 B/E A/E E
We will witness a race to be seen.

E9   E Emaj7 E6   B/E A/E E
There's a race at the local running track... no tickets to be sold.

E9   E   Emaj7 E6   A/B Amin/B E
There'll be no famous runners there... there'll be no winner's gold.

D/E   E D/E   E
But their determination to succeed will surely mean

D/E   E   C/D D7
That they will be part of... a race to be seen.

REFRAIN:

Gmaj7   Cmaj7   Gmaj7
Like the runners... we're all part of a race.

Cmaj7   Gmaj7
Some days you win... some days you fall.

Amin   Amin/G D7/F#   D7
  But if you never help yourself… then you'll never win at all.

Gmaj7   Cmaj7   Gmaj7   Cmaj7
  If you spend your life just dreaming… success won't come to you.

Gmaj7   Cmaj7   A/B B   E9 E Emaj7 E6 B/E A/E E
  Race to be seen and show the world… what you can do!

VERSE:
   E9   E Emaj7 E6   B/E   A/E E
   There's a race we should all attempt to win… but we don't always try.

   E9   E   Emaj7 E6   A/B Amin/B E
   If we give up hope for the future now… this race of ours will die.

GRAHAM, MARK AND MARIE:
           D/E   E   D/E   E
              For life is like a relay… we have our lap to run

      D/E   E C/D   D7
           Don't drop the baton… it's worth handing on!

REFRAIN:
      Gmaj7   Cmaj7   Gmaj7
         Like the runners… we're all part of a race.

         Cmaj7   Gmaj7
            Some days you win… some days you fall.

Amin   Amin/G D7/F#   D7
  But if you never help yourself… then you'll never win at all.

Gmaj7   Cmaj7   Gmaj7   Cmaj7
  If you spend your life just dreaming…success won't come to you.

Gmaj7   Cmaj7   A/B B   E9 E Emaj7
  Race to be seen and show the world… what you can do!

E6 A/B Amin/B E Emaj7   *E6 A/B Amin/B E*
  Race to be Seen.   *Race to be Seen.*

Teaching Resources

A Teachers' Resource pack, by Mark Wheeller and Tracy Dorrington, is available from the Salamander Street website.

See the Teaching Resources tab to download it.